# VENUS

## SEYMOUR SIMON

MORROW JUNIOR BOOKS
New York

PHOTO AND ART CREDITS
Photograph on pages 4-5, courtesy Janet C. Lindemann, M.D.;
photograph on pages 30-31, courtesy Johnson Space Center/NASA; all
other photographs, courtesy Jet Propulsion Laboratory/NASA. All artwork
by Ann Neumann.

The text type is 18 point Garamond Book (ITC).

Printed in Singapore at Tien Wah Press.

1  2  3  4  5  6  7  8  9  10

Library of Congress Cataloging-in-Publication Data
Simon, Seymour.
Venus / Seymour Simon.
p.    cm.
Summary: Describes the movements and physical features of the
planet Venus and recent findings about its climate and surface.
ISBN 0-688-10542-4. —ISBN 0-688-10543-2 (lib. bdg.)
1. Venus (Planet)—Juvenile literature.   [1. Venus (Planet)]
I. Title.
QB621.S56   1992
523.4′2—dc20   91-12171   CIP   AC

For Joyce

Venus is the brightest object in the night sky after the moon. Depending upon its orbit, Venus is the first "star" to appear in the western sky at sunset or the last to fade in the eastern sky at sunrise. Because it is so brilliant, it is sometimes called the Evening Star or the Morning Star. But Venus is not a star; it is a planet. The early Romans named the dazzling white planet Venus, after their goddess of love and beauty.

Venus is the second planet from the sun, between Mercury and our home planet, Earth. Its average distance from the sun is 68 million miles, about three-quarters of Earth's distance. Venus is 7,545 miles across, just a bit smaller than Earth; it has no moons.

Planets travel around the sun in paths called orbits. Earth takes 365 days to orbit the sun, or one Earth year. Venus is closer to the sun and travels around it more quickly. Its year is just 225 Earth days.

Our home planet takes 24 hours to rotate one time, one Earth day. Venus spins very slowly, taking 243 Earth days to spin just once. This means that on Venus a day is longer than a year.

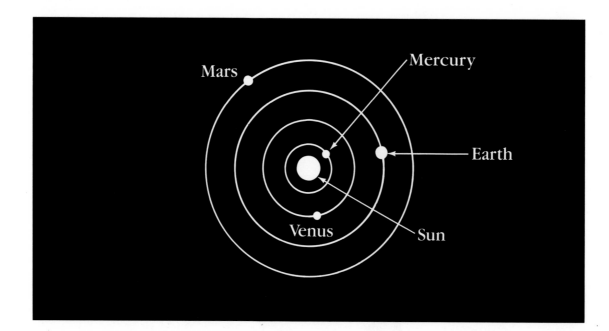

Venus rotates from east to west—the opposite of most other planets and moons in the Solar System. To an observer on Venus, the sun would rise in the west and daylight would last for 58 Earth days.

From Earth, Venus seems to change its shape just as our moon does. The shape varies from a slim crescent, to a thick slice, to full, and then back again to crescent. But, unlike the moon, Venus greatly changes its distance from us. When it is close to Earth, Venus appears much larger than when it is farthest away, on the other side of the sun. But the dense white clouds covering its surface reflect sunlight so well that Venus appears bright even when it is most distant.

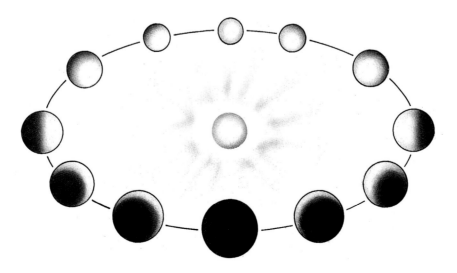

Venus is sometimes called Earth's sister planet because both are about the same size and have about the same mass and density. But conditions on Venus are very different from those on Earth. Venus is surrounded by a heavy atmosphere and is always hidden behind thick layers of clouds.

There is very little water on the planet, so the clouds around Venus are not made of water droplets like those on Earth but are composed of droplets of sulfuric acid. The layers of clouds extend from about fifteen to thirty miles above the surface.

Above and below the clouds, the atmosphere is clear. This view of Venus was taken by *Mariner 10* a day after it flew by Venus on its way to Mercury. The photo was processed with a blue filter to show cloud features clearly.

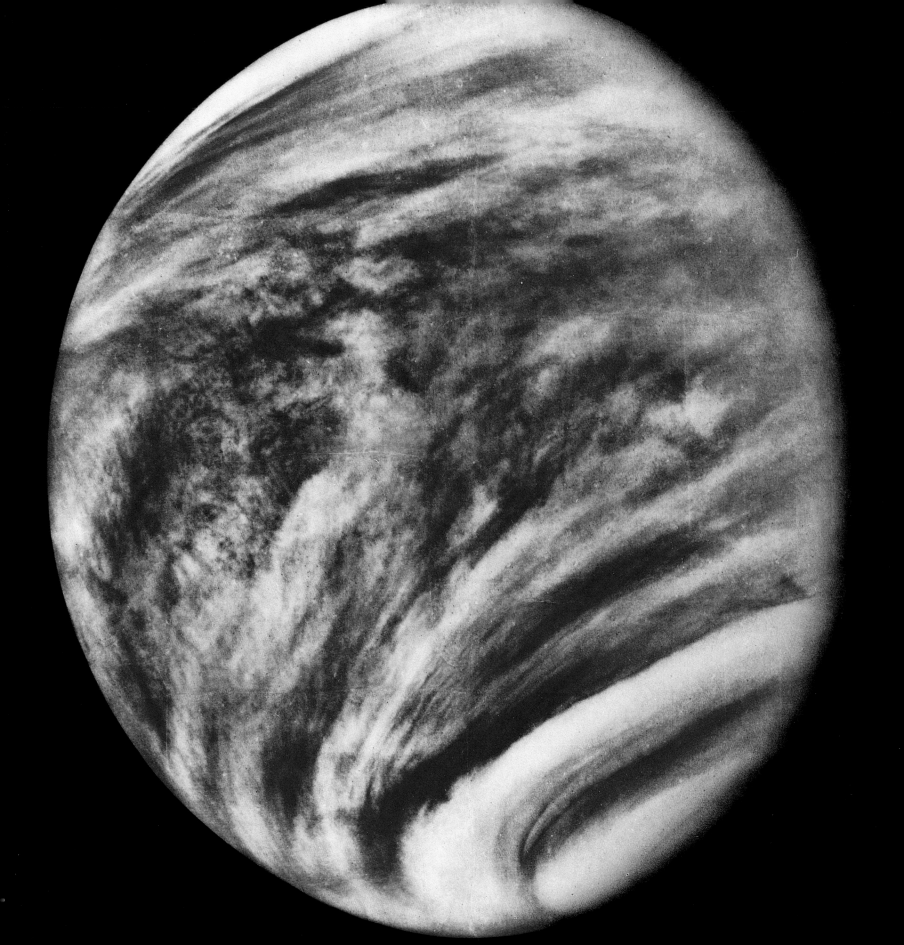

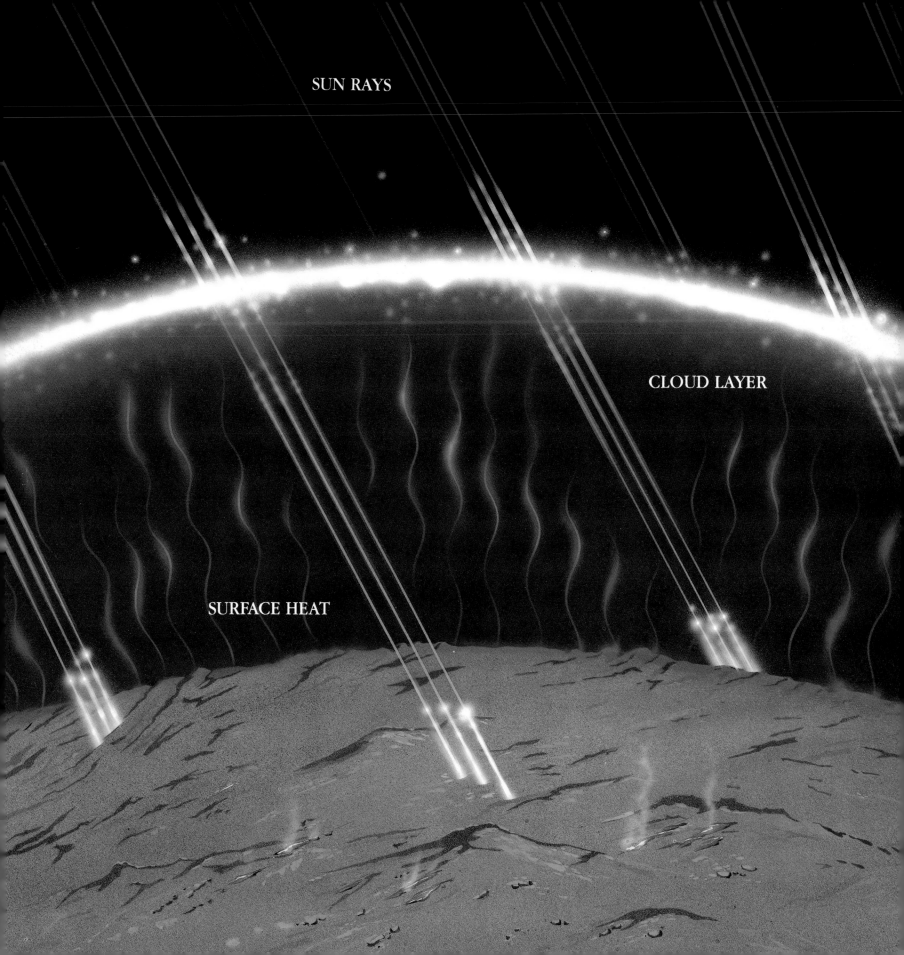

The surface of Venus is incredibly hot—as much as 900 degrees (F), day and night. That's hotter than a kitchen oven set to broiling temperature.

Although Venus is closer to the sun than is Earth, that isn't the only reason why the surface of Venus is scalding. Venus's thick atmosphere of carbon dioxide is mostly responsible for the intense heat. Sunlight passes through the atmosphere and heats up the rocky surface. The rocks radiate heat, but the dense atmosphere traps the heat and doesn't allow it to escape into space.

This is called the "greenhouse effect" because the glass windows in a greenhouse act the same way. The windows allow the sunlight to get through but then keep the heat from getting out. That's why the inside of a car becomes so hot when it sits in the sun. And that's why Venus is the hottest planet in the Solar System—even hotter than fiery Mercury.

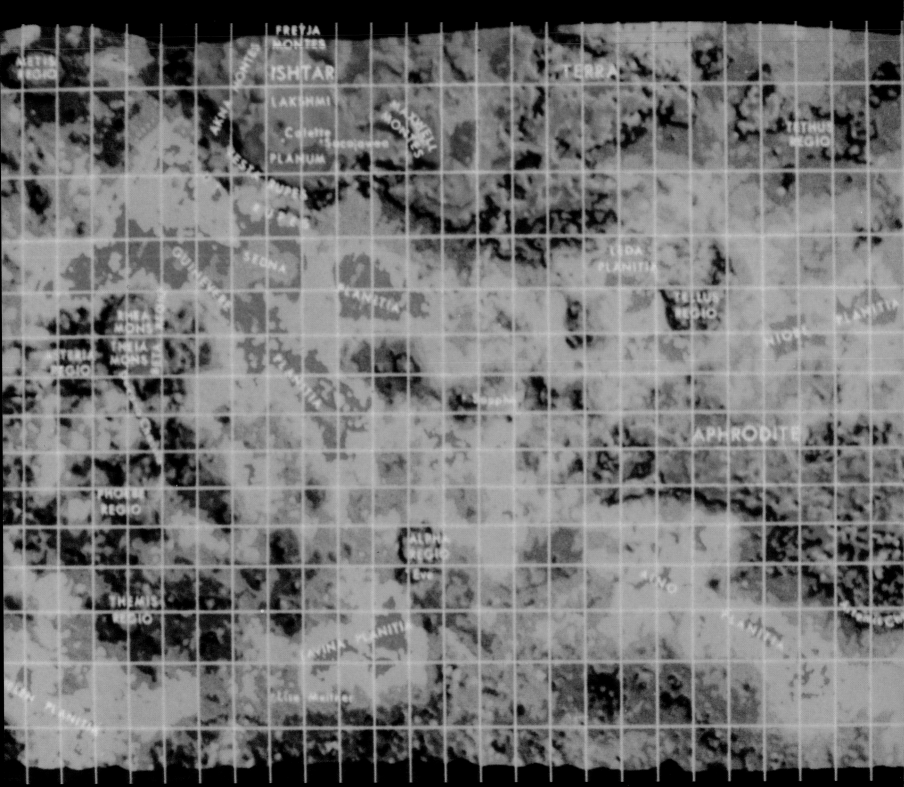

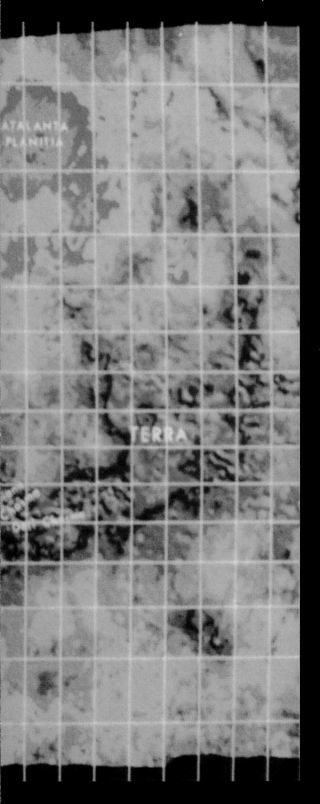

In 1980, the Pioneer Venus Orbiter spacecraft bounced radio waves off the planet to measure the heights of mountains and the depths of valleys to within a few hundred feet. The Orbiter radar survey was used to draw this color contour map.

About 70 percent of the surface of Venus is a vast desert of rolling plains (light blue). About 20 percent is lowlands (dark blue), and only about 10 percent of the planet's surface rises to form highlands (green, orange, and red). Two large highlands stand out like continents above the plains: Ishtar Terra to the north, about the size of Australia, and Aphrodite Terra in the middle, a region as large as Africa.

The main portion of Aphrodite Terra (from the Greek name for Venus) is shown in this global view of the planet made from the Orbiter radar map. Aphrodite is just south of Venus's equator. Mountains in Aphrodite lie to the east and west. The highlands are separated by deep and long valleys that drop down 15,000 feet below the surrounding ridges. On Aphrodite's southern edge is a giant circular basin more than a thousand miles across.

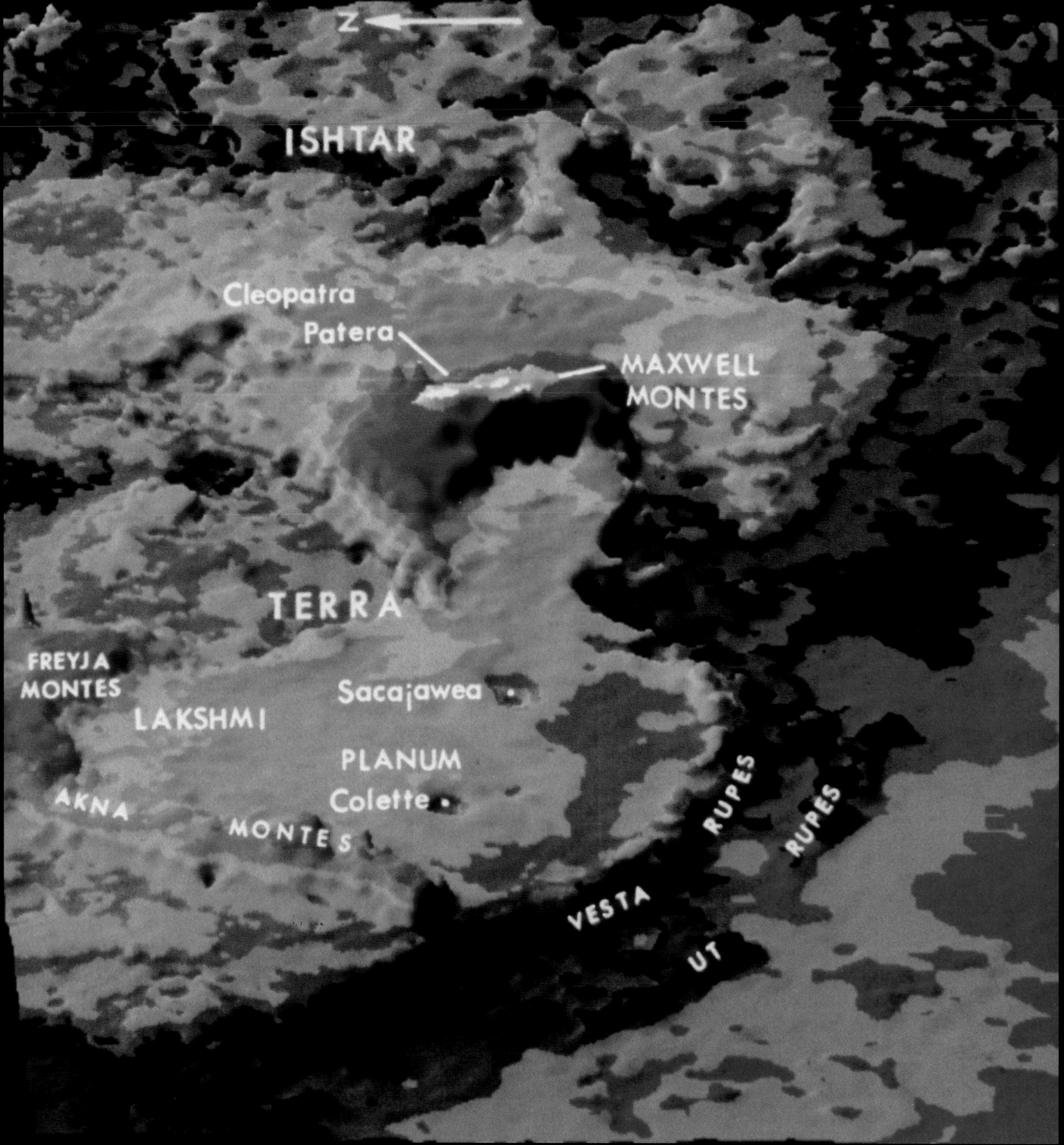

Z ⟶

ISHTAR

Cleopatra
Patera

MAXWELL
MONTES

TERRA

FREYJA
MONTES

Sacajawea

LAKSHMI

PLANUM

AKNA

Colette

MONTES

VESTA

RUPES

RUPES

UT

The Ishtar Terra region (from the Babylonian name for Venus) is a high plateau ringed by mountains. The tallest of these is the huge Maxwell Mountain, which rises thousands of feet higher than Mount Everest on Earth. It appears to be an immense volcano which is either extinct or not active at this time. At the summit of Maxwell is a volcanic crater nearly fifty miles wide.

From the mid-1960s to 1981, the Soviet Union launched a number of Venera spaceships to map and even land on Venus. Imagine one of the Venera landers dropping down through the atmosphere. First it plunged through 15 miles of thick, yellowish-white clouds of sulfuric acid blown by winds nearly 250 miles an hour. Beneath the clouds the lander passed through a dark, orange-red atmosphere with lightning crackling nearby. Once on the ground, the lander could operate for only about an hour before it was destroyed by the heat, acid droplets left by the clouds, and the crushing air pressure. The atmospheric pressure around the spacecraft was ninety times greater than air pressure at sea level on Earth.

The upper photo, taken by *Venera 13*, shows how the surface of Venus really looks. The orange color is the result of the clouds and atmosphere absorbing all of the blue color in the sun's light. The lower photo shows the same view as it would look in the sunlight on Earth.

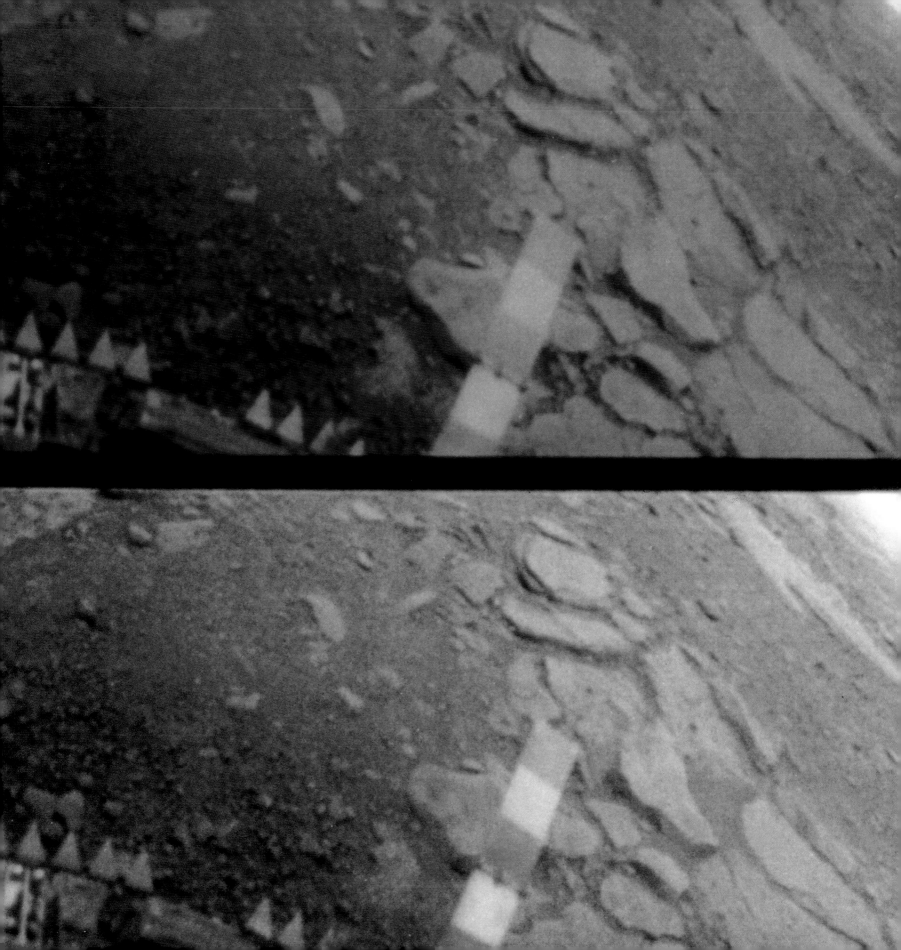

This image of the flat, rocky surface of Venus was taken by *Venera 14* in 1982. At the bottom of the photo, you can see parts of the lander, including a ladder-like arm and triangular "teeth" which steadied the spacecraft on

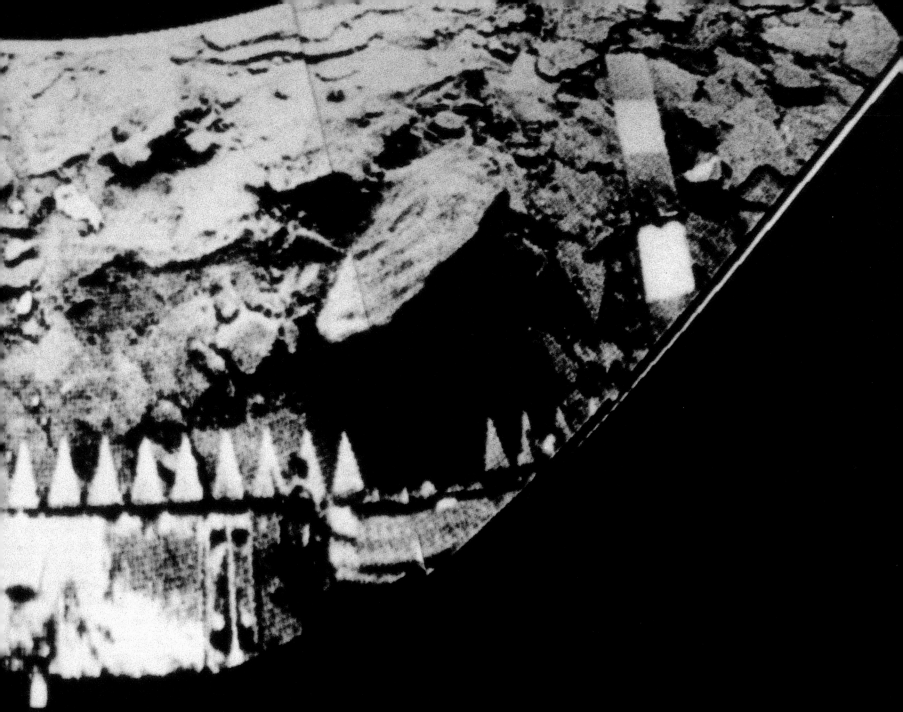

its descent. At the lower center are small pebbles. The large rock at the right is one to two feet across. The bedrock beneath the spacecraft may have come from lava flows in the past.

On August 10, 1990, NASA's *Magellan* spacecraft arrived in orbit around Venus. Every 3 hours and 9 minutes, the spacecraft completed one orbit and photographed a 16-mile-wide strip of the ground. Each day, *Magellan* orbited Venus nearly eight times and sent back more images than all the previous missions put together.

This photo of the *Magellan* spacecraft with Earth in the background was taken by an astronaut with a handheld camera on board the *Atlantis* space shuttle. The astronaut carried the film back to Earth at the end of the flight, and the photo was developed. Sending back images from *Magellan* was much more difficult. *Magellan* used cloud-piercing radar to collect information about the surface of the planet. The spacecraft later turned its antenna toward Earth and sent back radio signals containing the data. The radio signals were received by antennas on Earth, sent to computers, and processed into photos of the planet. The images *Magellan* took show surface details the size of a football field, ten times smaller than any previous radar photos.

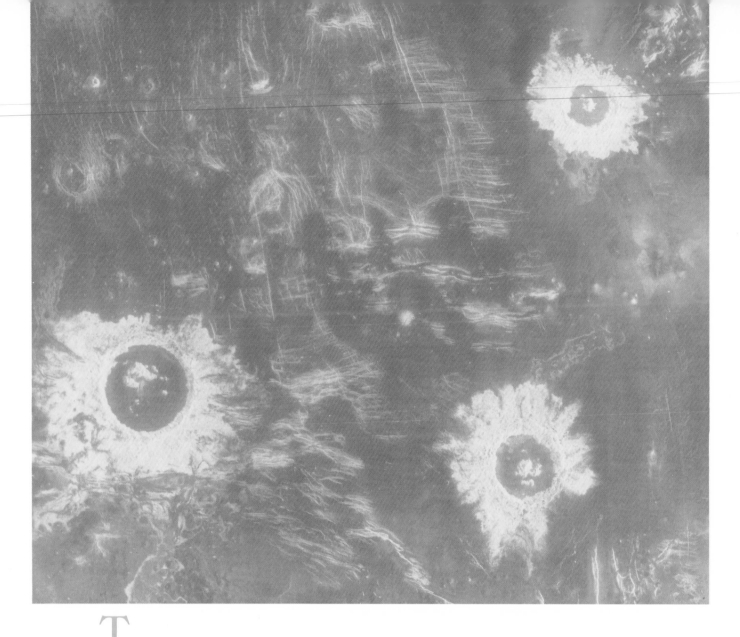

This radar map, made from thirty *Magellan* photos, shows a 300-mile strip in the Southern Hemisphere. Three large meteorite-impact craters, each about thirty miles wide, resemble impact craters on Earth, the moon, and Mars. The craters show central peaks and are surrounded by rocky material flung out by the impact.

Seven domed hills can be seen in this image of one of the main volcanic areas. These pancake-shaped domes are about a half mile high and ten miles wide. They look like volcanic domes found on Earth and may have been formed by thick lava pouring out of volcanic vents and flowing along the ground. Most of the surface of Venus appears to be old, and not much seems to have happened since early volcanic activity hundreds of millions of years ago.

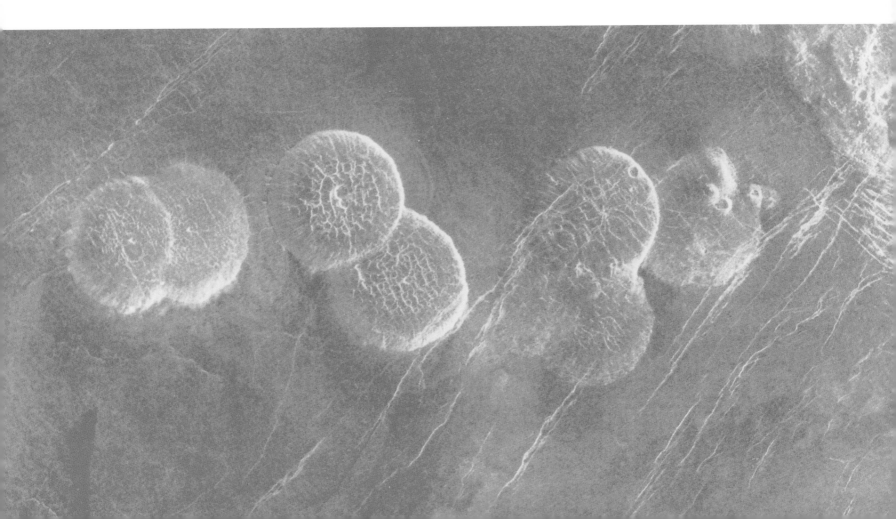

The mountains in this photo probably were formed by huge blocks of molten rock rising up from inside Venus. Like Earth, Venus has a molten core. The dark and bright streaks are lava flows that poured out of volcanic vents long ago and hardened along the ground. The black strips across the image are areas where radar information was not collected. *Magellan* will fill in the gaps during the next few years.

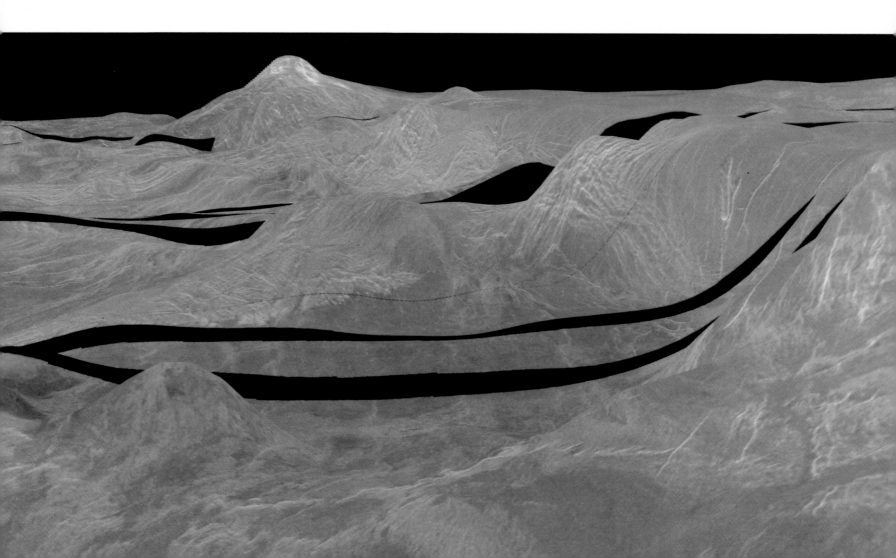

This photo shows two sets of lines that cross almost at right angles to each other. The fainter ones are about a half mile apart and stretch for miles. The bright ones are less regular. These strange lines are a puzzle to scientists, who believe they are breaks or faults in the ground of some kind. Such features have never been seen before on any other planet.

$M$*agellan*'s photos show us that Venus has no craters smaller than about four miles across. That's because the planet's atmosphere is so dense that it stops smaller incoming meteors before they can hit the ground and make the craters.

This radar photo shows part of the 20-mile-wide Golubkina crater. The banked inner walls and central peak look like those of impact craters seen on Earth, the moon, and Mars. The crater may have once been flooded by lava that hardened into a flat, smooth floor.

For centuries, people thought that Venus was a steaming ocean world of giant swamps and huge animals. The truth is even stranger—we now know that Venus is a scorching desert with temperatures hot enough to melt lead. Venus has no oceans and no life. How did it end up being so different from its "sister planet," Earth? And what can Venus teach us about the danger of too much "greenhouse warming"? These are just some of the questions *Magellan* may help answer.